T0162641

MY PERSONAL
COMPUTER
DATABASE

MY PERSONAL
COMPUTER
DATABASE

SANDRA NELSON

MY PERSONAL COMPUTER DATABASE

Copyright © 2016 Sandra Nelson.

All rights reserved. No part of this book may be used or reproduced by any means, graphic, electronic, or mechanical, including photocopying, recording, taping or by any information storage retrieval system without the written permission of the author except in the case of brief quotations embodied in critical articles and reviews.

iUniverse books may be ordered through booksellers or by contacting:

iUniverse
1663 Liberty Drive
Bloomington, IN 47403
www.iuniverse.com
1-800-Authors (1-800-288-4677)

Because of the dynamic nature of the Internet, any web addresses or links contained in this book may have changed since publication and may no longer be valid. The views expressed in this work are solely those of the author and do not necessarily reflect the views of the publisher, and the publisher hereby disclaims any responsibility for them.

Any people depicted in stock imagery provided by Thinkstock are models, and such images are being used for illustrative purposes only. Certain stock imagery © Thinkstock.

ISBN: 978-1-4917-8946-9 (sc)
ISBN: 978-1-4917-8945-2 (e)

Print information available on the last page.

iUniverse rev. date: 02/03/2016

A

Company Name	
Website	
Username	Password
Email	
Phone	Fax

Company Name	
Website	
Username	Password
Email	
Phone	Fax

Company Name	
Website	
Username	Password
Email	
Phone	Fax

Company Name	
Website	
Username	Password
Email	
Phone	Fax

Company Name	
Website	
Username	Password
Email	
Phone	Fax

Company Name	
Website	
Username	Password
Email	
Phone	Fax

A

Company Name	
Website	
Username	Password
Email	
Phone	Fax

Company Name	
Website	
Username	Password
Email	
Phone	Fax

Company Name	
Website	
Username	Password
Email	
Phone	Fax

Company Name	
Website	
Username	Password
Email	
Phone	Fax

Company Name	
Website	
Username	Password
Email	
Phone	Fax

Company Name	
Website	
Username	Password
Email	
Phone	Fax

A

Company Name	
Website	
Username	Password
Email	
Phone	Fax

Company Name	
Website	
Username	Password
Email	
Phone	Fax

Company Name	
Website	
Username	Password
Email	
Phone	Fax

Company Name	
Website	
Username	Password
Email	
Phone	Fax

Company Name	
Website	
Username	Password
Email	
Phone	Fax

Company Name	
Website	
Username	Password
Email	
Phone	Fax

A

Company Name	
Website	
Username	Password
Email	
Phone	Fax

Company Name	
Website	
Username	Password
Email	
Phone	Fax

Company Name	
Website	
Username	Password
Email	
Phone	Fax

Company Name	
Website	
Username	Password
Email	
Phone	Fax

Company Name	
Website	
Username	Password
Email	
Phone	Fax

Company Name	
Website	
Username	Password
Email	
Phone	Fax

B

Company Name	
Website	
Username	Password
Email	
Phone	Fax
Company Name	
Website	
Username	Password
Email	
Phone	Fax
Company Name	
Website	
Username	Password
Email	
Phone	Fax
Company Name	
Website	
Username	Password
Email	
Phone	Fax
Company Name	
Website	
Username	Password
Email	
Phone	Fax
Company Name	
Website	
Username	Password
Email	
Phone	Fax

Company Name	
Website	
Username	Password
Email	
Phone	Fax
Company Name	
Website	
Username	Password
Email	
Phone	Fax
Company Name	
Website	
Username	Password
Email	
Phone	Fax
Company Name	
Website	
Username	Password
Email	
Phone	Fax
Company Name	
Website	
Username	Password
Email	
Phone	Fax
Company Name	
Website	
Username	Password
Email	
Phone	Fax

B

Company Name	
Website	
Username	Password
Email	
Phone	Fax

Company Name	
Website	
Username	Password
Email	
Phone	Fax

Company Name	
Website	
Username	Password
Email	
Phone	Fax

Company Name	
Website	
Username	Password
Email	
Phone	Fax

Company Name	
Website	
Username	Password
Email	
Phone	Fax

Company Name	
Website	
Username	Password
Email	
Phone	Fax

B

Company Name	
Website	
Username	Password
Email	
Phone	Fax
Company Name	
Website	
Username	Password
Email	
Phone	Fax
Company Name	
Website	
Username	Password
Email	
Phone	Fax
Company Name	
Website	
Username	Password
Email	
Phone	Fax
Company Name	
Website	
Username	Password
Email	
Phone	Fax
Company Name	
Website	
Username	Password
Email	
Phone	Fax

C

Company Name	
Website	
Username	Password
Email	
Phone	Fax
Company Name	
Website	
Username	Password
Email	
Phone	Fax
Company Name	
Website	
Username	Password
Email	
Phone	Fax
Company Name	
Website	
Username	Password
Email	
Phone	Fax
Company Name	
Website	
Username	Password
Email	
Phone	Fax
Company Name	
Website	
Username	Password
Email	
Phone	Fax

C

Company Name	
Website	
Username	Password
Email	
Phone	Fax

Company Name	
Website	
Username	Password
Email	
Phone	Fax

Company Name	
Website	
Username	Password
Email	
Phone	Fax

Company Name	
Website	
Username	Password
Email	
Phone	Fax

Company Name	
Website	
Username	Password
Email	
Phone	Fax

Company Name	
Website	
Username	Password
Email	
Phone	Fax

C

Company Name	
Website	
Username	Password
Email	
Phone	Fax
Company Name	
Website	
Username	Password
Email	
Phone	Fax
Company Name	
Website	
Username	Password
Email	
Phone	Fax
Company Name	
Website	
Username	Password
Email	
Phone	Fax
Company Name	
Website	
Username	Password
Email	
Phone	Fax
Company Name	
Website	
Username	Password
Email	
Phone	Fax

C

Company Name	
Website	
Username	Password
Email	
Phone	Fax
Company Name	
Website	
Username	Password
Email	
Phone	Fax
Company Name	
Website	
Username	Password
Email	
Phone	Fax
Company Name	
Website	
Username	Password
Email	
Phone	Fax
Company Name	
Website	
Username	Password
Email	
Phone	Fax
Company Name	
Website	
Username	Password
Email	
Phone	Fax

D

Company Name	
Website	
Username	Password
Email	
Phone	Fax

Company Name	
Website	
Username	Password
Email	
Phone	Fax

Company Name	
Website	
Username	Password
Email	
Phone	Fax

Company Name	
Website	
Username	Password
Email	
Phone	Fax

Company Name	
Website	
Username	Password
Email	
Phone	Fax

Company Name	
Website	
Username	Password
Email	
Phone	Fax

D

Company Name	
Website	
Username	Password
Email	
Phone	Fax

Company Name	
Website	
Username	Password
Email	
Phone	Fax

Company Name	
Website	
Username	Password
Email	
Phone	Fax

Company Name	
Website	
Username	Password
Email	
Phone	Fax

Company Name	
Website	
Username	Password
Email	
Phone	Fax

Company Name	
Website	
Username	Password
Email	
Phone	Fax

D

Company Name

Website

Username   Password

Email

Phone   Fax

Company Name

Website

Username   Password

Email

Phone   Fax

Company Name

Website

Username   Password

Email

Phone   Fax

Company Name

Website

Username   Password

Email

Phone   Fax

Company Name

Website

Username   Password

Email

Phone   Fax

Company Name

Website

Username   Password

Email

Phone   Fax

D

Company Name	
Website	
Username	Password
Email	
Phone	Fax

Company Name	
Website	
Username	Password
Email	
Phone	Fax

Company Name	
Website	
Username	Password
Email	
Phone	Fax

Company Name	
Website	
Username	Password
Email	
Phone	Fax

Company Name	
Website	
Username	Password
Email	
Phone	Fax

Company Name	
Website	
Username	Password
Email	
Phone	Fax

E

Company Name	
Website	
Username	Password
Email	
Phone	Fax

Company Name	
Website	
Username	Password
Email	
Phone	Fax

Company Name	
Website	
Username	Password
Email	
Phone	Fax

Company Name	
Website	
Username	Password
Email	
Phone	Fax

Company Name	
Website	
Username	Password
Email	
Phone	Fax

Company Name	
Website	
Username	Password
Email	
Phone	Fax

E

Company Name	
Website	
Username	Password
Email	
Phone	Fax

Company Name	
Website	
Username	Password
Email	
Phone	Fax

Company Name	
Website	
Username	Password
Email	
Phone	Fax

Company Name	
Website	
Username	Password
Email	
Phone	Fax

Company Name	
Website	
Username	Password
Email	
Phone	Fax

Company Name	
Website	
Username	Password
Email	
Phone	Fax

E

Company Name	
Website	
Username	Password
Email	
Phone	Fax

Company Name	
Website	
Username	Password
Email	
Phone	Fax

Company Name	
Website	
Username	Password
Email	
Phone	Fax

Company Name	
Website	
Username	Password
Email	
Phone	Fax

Company Name	
Website	
Username	Password
Email	
Phone	Fax

Company Name	
Website	
Username	Password
Email	
Phone	Fax

E

Company Name	
Website	
Username	Password
Email	
Phone	Fax
Company Name	
Website	
Username	Password
Email	
Phone	Fax
Company Name	
Website	
Username	Password
Email	
Phone	Fax
Company Name	
Website	
Username	Password
Email	
Phone	Fax
Company Name	
Website	
Username	Password
Email	
Phone	Fax
Company Name	
Website	
Username	Password
Email	
Phone	Fax

F

Company Name

Website

Username   Password

Email

Phone   Fax

Company Name

Website

Username   Password

Email

Phone   Fax

Company Name

Website

Username   Password

Email

Phone   Fax

Company Name

Website

Username   Password

Email

Phone   Fax

Company Name

Website

Username   Password

Email

Phone   Fax

Company Name

Website

Username   Password

Email

Phone   Fax

F

Company Name	
Website	
Username	Password
Email	
Phone	Fax

Company Name	
Website	
Username	Password
Email	
Phone	Fax

Company Name	
Website	
Username	Password
Email	
Phone	Fax

Company Name	
Website	
Username	Password
Email	
Phone	Fax

Company Name	
Website	
Username	Password
Email	
Phone	Fax

Company Name	
Website	
Username	Password
Email	
Phone	Fax

F

Company Name

Website

Username   Password

Email

Phone   Fax

Company Name

Website

Username   Password

Email

Phone   Fax

Company Name

Website

Username   Password

Email

Phone   Fax

Company Name

Website

Username   Password

Email

Phone   Fax

Company Name

Website

Username   Password

Email

Phone   Fax

Company Name

Website

Username   Password

Email

Phone   Fax

Company Name	
Website	
Username	Password
Email	
Phone	Fax
Company Name	
Website	
Username	Password
Email	
Phone	Fax
Company Name	
Website	
Username	Password
Email	
Phone	Fax
Company Name	
Website	
Username	Password
Email	
Phone	Fax
Company Name	
Website	
Username	Password
Email	
Phone	Fax
Company Name	
Website	
Username	Password
Email	
Phone	Fax

G

Company Name	
Website	
Username	Password
Email	
Phone	Fax
Company Name	
Website	
Username	Password
Email	
Phone	Fax
Company Name	
Website	
Username	Password
Email	
Phone	Fax
Company Name	
Website	
Username	Password
Email	
Phone	Fax
Company Name	
Website	
Username	Password
Email	
Phone	Fax
Company Name	
Website	
Username	Password
Email	
Phone	Fax

Company Name	
Website	
Username	Password
Email	
Phone	Fax

Company Name	
Website	
Username	Password
Email	
Phone	Fax

Company Name	
Website	
Username	Password
Email	
Phone	Fax

Company Name	
Website	
Username	Password
Email	
Phone	Fax

Company Name	
Website	
Username	Password
Email	
Phone	Fax

Company Name	
Website	
Username	Password
Email	
Phone	Fax

G

Company Name	
Website	
Username	Password
Email	
Phone	Fax
Company Name	
Website	
Username	Password
Email	
Phone	Fax
Company Name	
Website	
Username	Password
Email	
Phone	Fax
Company Name	
Website	
Username	Password
Email	
Phone	Fax
Company Name	
Website	
Username	Password
Email	
Phone	Fax
Company Name	
Website	
Username	Password
Email	
Phone	Fax

G

Company Name	
Website	
Username	Password
Email	
Phone	Fax

Company Name	
Website	
Username	Password
Email	
Phone	Fax

Company Name	
Website	
Username	Password
Email	
Phone	Fax

Company Name	
Website	
Username	Password
Email	
Phone	Fax

Company Name	
Website	
Username	Password
Email	
Phone	Fax

Company Name	
Website	
Username	Password
Email	
Phone	Fax

H

Company Name

Website

Username   Password

Email

Phone   Fax

Company Name

Website

Username   Password

Email

Phone   Fax

Company Name

Website

Username   Password

Email

Phone   Fax

Company Name

Website

Username   Password

Email

Phone   Fax

Company Name

Website

Username   Password

Email

Phone   Fax

Company Name

Website

Username   Password

Email

Phone   Fax

H

Company Name	
Website	
Username	Password
Email	
Phone	Fax

Company Name	
Website	
Username	Password
Email	
Phone	Fax

Company Name	
Website	
Username	Password
Email	
Phone	Fax

Company Name	
Website	
Username	Password
Email	
Phone	Fax

Company Name	
Website	
Username	Password
Email	
Phone	Fax

Company Name	
Website	
Username	Password
Email	
Phone	Fax

H

Company Name

Website

Username   Password

Email

Phone   Fax

Company Name

Website

Username   Password

Email

Phone   Fax

Company Name

Website

Username   Password

Email

Phone   Fax

Company Name

Website

Username   Password

Email

Phone   Fax

Company Name

Website

Username   Password

Email

Phone   Fax

Company Name

Website

Username   Password

Email

Phone   Fax

Company Name	
Website	
Username	Password
Email	
Phone	Fax

Company Name	
Website	
Username	Password
Email	
Phone	Fax

Company Name	
Website	
Username	Password
Email	
Phone	Fax

Company Name	
Website	
Username	Password
Email	
Phone	Fax

Company Name	
Website	
Username	Password
Email	
Phone	Fax

Company Name	
Website	
Username	Password
Email	
Phone	Fax

I

Company Name	
Website	
Username	Password
Email	
Phone	Fax

Company Name	
Website	
Username	Password
Email	
Phone	Fax

Company Name	
Website	
Username	Password
Email	
Phone	Fax

Company Name	
Website	
Username	Password
Email	
Phone	Fax

Company Name	
Website	
Username	Password
Email	
Phone	Fax

Company Name	
Website	
Username	Password
Email	
Phone	Fax

Company Name	
Website	
Username	Password
Email	
Phone	Fax
Company Name	
Website	
Username	Password
Email	
Phone	Fax
Company Name	
Website	
Username	Password
Email	
Phone	Fax
Company Name	
Website	
Username	Password
Email	
Phone	Fax
Company Name	
Website	
Username	Password
Email	
Phone	Fax
Company Name	
Website	
Username	Password
Email	
Phone	Fax

I

Company Name	
Website	
Username	Password
Email	
Phone	Fax
Company Name	
Website	
Username	Password
Email	
Phone	Fax
Company Name	
Website	
Username	Password
Email	
Phone	Fax
Company Name	
Website	
Username	Password
Email	
Phone	Fax
Company Name	
Website	
Username	Password
Email	
Phone	Fax
Company Name	
Website	
Username	Password
Email	
Phone	Fax

Company Name	
Website	
Username	Password
Email	
Phone	Fax

Company Name	
Website	
Username	Password
Email	
Phone	Fax

Company Name	
Website	
Username	Password
Email	
Phone	Fax

Company Name	
Website	
Username	Password
Email	
Phone	Fax

Company Name	
Website	
Username	Password
Email	
Phone	Fax

Company Name	
Website	
Username	Password
Email	
Phone	Fax

J

Company Name	
Website	
Username	Password
Email	
Phone	Fax

Company Name	
Website	
Username	Password
Email	
Phone	Fax

Company Name	
Website	
Username	Password
Email	
Phone	Fax

Company Name	
Website	
Username	Password
Email	
Phone	Fax

Company Name	
Website	
Username	Password
Email	
Phone	Fax

Company Name	
Website	
Username	Password
Email	
Phone	Fax

J

Company Name	
Website	
Username	Password
Email	
Phone	Fax

Company Name	
Website	
Username	Password
Email	
Phone	Fax

Company Name	
Website	
Username	Password
Email	
Phone	Fax

Company Name	
Website	
Username	Password
Email	
Phone	Fax

Company Name	
Website	
Username	Password
Email	
Phone	Fax

Company Name	
Website	
Username	Password
Email	
Phone	Fax

J

Company Name	
Website	
Username	Password
Email	
Phone	Fax
Company Name	
Website	
Username	Password
Email	
Phone	Fax
Company Name	
Website	
Username	Password
Email	
Phone	Fax
Company Name	
Website	
Username	Password
Email	
Phone	Fax
Company Name	
Website	
Username	Password
Email	
Phone	Fax
Company Name	
Website	
Username	Password
Email	
Phone	Fax

J

Company Name	
Website	
Username	Password
Email	
Phone	Fax

Company Name	
Website	
Username	Password
Email	
Phone	Fax

Company Name	
Website	
Username	Password
Email	
Phone	Fax

Company Name	
Website	
Username	Password
Email	
Phone	Fax

Company Name	
Website	
Username	Password
Email	
Phone	Fax

Company Name	
Website	
Username	Password
Email	
Phone	Fax

K

Company Name	
Website	
Username	Password
Email	
Phone	Fax

Company Name	
Website	
Username	Password
Email	
Phone	Fax

Company Name	
Website	
Username	Password
Email	
Phone	Fax

Company Name	
Website	
Username	Password
Email	
Phone	Fax

Company Name	
Website	
Username	Password
Email	
Phone	Fax

Company Name	
Website	
Username	Password
Email	
Phone	Fax

K

Company Name	
Website	
Username	Password
Email	
Phone	Fax

Company Name	
Website	
Username	Password
Email	
Phone	Fax

Company Name	
Website	
Username	Password
Email	
Phone	Fax

Company Name	
Website	
Username	Password
Email	
Phone	Fax

Company Name	
Website	
Username	Password
Email	
Phone	Fax

Company Name	
Website	
Username	Password
Email	
Phone	Fax

K

Company Name	
Website	
Username	Password
Email	
Phone	Fax

Company Name	
Website	
Username	Password
Email	
Phone	Fax

Company Name	
Website	
Username	Password
Email	
Phone	Fax

Company Name	
Website	
Username	Password
Email	
Phone	Fax

Company Name	
Website	
Username	Password
Email	
Phone	Fax

Company Name	
Website	
Username	Password
Email	
Phone	Fax

K

Company Name	
Website	
Username	Password
Email	
Phone	Fax

Company Name	
Website	
Username	Password
Email	
Phone	Fax

Company Name	
Website	
Username	Password
Email	
Phone	Fax

Company Name	
Website	
Username	Password
Email	
Phone	Fax

Company Name	
Website	
Username	Password
Email	
Phone	Fax

Company Name	
Website	
Username	Password
Email	
Phone	Fax

L

Company Name

Website

Username   Password

Email

Phone   Fax

Company Name

Website

Username   Password

Email

Phone   Fax

Company Name

Website

Username   Password

Email

Phone   Fax

Company Name

Website

Username   Password

Email

Phone   Fax

Company Name

Website

Username   Password

Email

Phone   Fax

Company Name

Website

Username   Password

Email

Phone   Fax

L

Company Name	
Website	
Username	Password
Email	
Phone	Fax

Company Name	
Website	
Username	Password
Email	
Phone	Fax

Company Name	
Website	
Username	Password
Email	
Phone	Fax

Company Name	
Website	
Username	Password
Email	
Phone	Fax

Company Name	
Website	
Username	Password
Email	
Phone	Fax

Company Name	
Website	
Username	Password
Email	
Phone	Fax

L

Company Name	
Website	
Username	Password
Email	
Phone	Fax

Company Name	
Website	
Username	Password
Email	
Phone	Fax

Company Name	
Website	
Username	Password
Email	
Phone	Fax

Company Name	
Website	
Username	Password
Email	
Phone	Fax

Company Name	
Website	
Username	Password
Email	
Phone	Fax

Company Name	
Website	
Username	Password
Email	
Phone	Fax

L

Company Name	
Website	
Username	Password
Email	
Phone	Fax
Company Name	
Website	
Username	Password
Email	
Phone	Fax
Company Name	
Website	
Username	Password
Email	
Phone	Fax
Company Name	
Website	
Username	Password
Email	
Phone	Fax
Company Name	
Website	
Username	Password
Email	
Phone	Fax
Company Name	
Website	
Username	Password
Email	
Phone	Fax

M

Company Name	
Website	
Username	Password
Email	
Phone	Fax

Company Name	
Website	
Username	Password
Email	
Phone	Fax

Company Name	
Website	
Username	Password
Email	
Phone	Fax

Company Name	
Website	
Username	Password
Email	
Phone	Fax

Company Name	
Website	
Username	Password
Email	
Phone	Fax

Company Name	
Website	
Username	Password
Email	
Phone	Fax

M

Company Name	
Website	
Username	Password
Email	
Phone	Fax

Company Name	
Website	
Username	Password
Email	
Phone	Fax

Company Name	
Website	
Username	Password
Email	
Phone	Fax

Company Name	
Website	
Username	Password
Email	
Phone	Fax

Company Name	
Website	
Username	Password
Email	
Phone	Fax

Company Name	
Website	
Username	Password
Email	
Phone	Fax

M

Company Name	
Website	
Username	Password
Email	
Phone	Fax
Company Name	
Website	
Username	Password
Email	
Phone	Fax
Company Name	
Website	
Username	Password
Email	
Phone	Fax
Company Name	
Website	
Username	Password
Email	
Phone	Fax
Company Name	
Website	
Username	Password
Email	
Phone	Fax
Company Name	
Website	
Username	Password
Email	
Phone	Fax

M

Company Name	
Website	
Username	Password
Email	
Phone	Fax

Company Name	
Website	
Username	Password
Email	
Phone	Fax

Company Name	
Website	
Username	Password
Email	
Phone	Fax

Company Name	
Website	
Username	Password
Email	
Phone	Fax

Company Name	
Website	
Username	Password
Email	
Phone	Fax

Company Name	
Website	
Username	Password
Email	
Phone	Fax

N

Company Name	
Website	
Username	Password
Email	
Phone	Fax
Company Name	
Website	
Username	Password
Email	
Phone	Fax
Company Name	
Website	
Username	Password
Email	
Phone	Fax
Company Name	
Website	
Username	Password
Email	
Phone	Fax
Company Name	
Website	
Username	Password
Email	
Phone	Fax
Company Name	
Website	
Username	Password
Email	
Phone	Fax

Company Name	
Website	
Username	Password
Email	
Phone	Fax

Company Name	
Website	
Username	Password
Email	
Phone	Fax

Company Name	
Website	
Username	Password
Email	
Phone	Fax

Company Name	
Website	
Username	Password
Email	
Phone	Fax

Company Name	
Website	
Username	Password
Email	
Phone	Fax

Company Name	
Website	
Username	Password
Email	
Phone	Fax

N

Company Name

Website

Username   Password

Email

Phone   Fax

Company Name

Website

Username   Password

Email

Phone   Fax

Company Name

Website

Username   Password

Email

Phone   Fax

Company Name

Website

Username   Password

Email

Phone   Fax

Company Name

Website

Username   Password

Email

Phone   Fax

Company Name

Website

Username   Password

Email

Phone   Fax

N

Company Name	
Website	
Username	Password
Email	
Phone	Fax

Company Name	
Website	
Username	Password
Email	
Phone	Fax

Company Name	
Website	
Username	Password
Email	
Phone	Fax

Company Name	
Website	
Username	Password
Email	
Phone	Fax

Company Name	
Website	
Username	Password
Email	
Phone	Fax

Company Name	
Website	
Username	Password
Email	
Phone	Fax

O

Company Name	
Website	
Username	Password
Email	
Phone	Fax
Company Name	
Website	
Username	Password
Email	
Phone	Fax
Company Name	
Website	
Username	Password
Email	
Phone	Fax
Company Name	
Website	
Username	Password
Email	
Phone	Fax
Company Name	
Website	
Username	Password
Email	
Phone	Fax
Company Name	
Website	
Username	Password
Email	
Phone	Fax

O

Company Name	
Website	
Username	Password
Email	
Phone	Fax
Company Name	
Website	
Username	Password
Email	
Phone	Fax
Company Name	
Website	
Username	Password
Email	
Phone	Fax
Company Name	
Website	
Username	Password
Email	
Phone	Fax
Company Name	
Website	
Username	Password
Email	
Phone	Fax
Company Name	
Website	
Username	Password
Email	
Phone	Fax

O

Company Name	
Website	
Username	Password
Email	
Phone	Fax

Company Name	
Website	
Username	Password
Email	
Phone	Fax

Company Name	
Website	
Username	Password
Email	
Phone	Fax

Company Name	
Website	
Username	Password
Email	
Phone	Fax

Company Name	
Website	
Username	Password
Email	
Phone	Fax

Company Name	
Website	
Username	Password
Email	
Phone	Fax

O

Company Name	
Website	
Username	Password
Email	
Phone	Fax

Company Name	
Website	
Username	Password
Email	
Phone	Fax

Company Name	
Website	
Username	Password
Email	
Phone	Fax

Company Name	
Website	
Username	Password
Email	
Phone	Fax

Company Name	
Website	
Username	Password
Email	
Phone	Fax

Company Name	
Website	
Username	Password
Email	
Phone	Fax

P

Company Name	
Website	
Username	Password
Email	
Phone	Fax

Company Name	
Website	
Username	Password
Email	
Phone	Fax

Company Name	
Website	
Username	Password
Email	
Phone	Fax

Company Name	
Website	
Username	Password
Email	
Phone	Fax

Company Name	
Website	
Username	Password
Email	
Phone	Fax

Company Name	
Website	
Username	Password
Email	
Phone	Fax

P

Company Name	
Website	
Username	Password
Email	
Phone	Fax

Company Name	
Website	
Username	Password
Email	
Phone	Fax

Company Name	
Website	
Username	Password
Email	
Phone	Fax

Company Name	
Website	
Username	Password
Email	
Phone	Fax

Company Name	
Website	
Username	Password
Email	
Phone	Fax

Company Name	
Website	
Username	Password
Email	
Phone	Fax

P

Company Name	
Website	
Username	Password
Email	
Phone	Fax

Company Name	
Website	
Username	Password
Email	
Phone	Fax

Company Name	
Website	
Username	Password
Email	
Phone	Fax

Company Name	
Website	
Username	Password
Email	
Phone	Fax

Company Name	
Website	
Username	Password
Email	
Phone	Fax

Company Name	
Website	
Username	Password
Email	
Phone	Fax

P

Company Name	
Website	
Username	Password
Email	
Phone	Fax

Company Name	
Website	
Username	Password
Email	
Phone	Fax

Company Name	
Website	
Username	Password
Email	
Phone	Fax

Company Name	
Website	
Username	Password
Email	
Phone	Fax

Company Name	
Website	
Username	Password
Email	
Phone	Fax

Company Name	
Website	
Username	Password
Email	
Phone	Fax

Q

Company Name	
Website	
Username	Password
Email	
Phone	Fax
Company Name	
Website	
Username	Password
Email	
Phone	Fax
Company Name	
Website	
Username	Password
Email	
Phone	Fax
Company Name	
Website	
Username	Password
Email	
Phone	Fax
Company Name	
Website	
Username	Password
Email	
Phone	Fax
Company Name	
Website	
Username	Password
Email	
Phone	Fax

Q

Company Name	
Website	
Username	Password
Email	
Phone	Fax
Company Name	
Website	
Username	Password
Email	
Phone	Fax
Company Name	
Website	
Username	Password
Email	
Phone	Fax
Company Name	
Website	
Username	Password
Email	
Phone	Fax
Company Name	
Website	
Username	Password
Email	
Phone	Fax
Company Name	
Website	
Username	Password
Email	
Phone	Fax

Q

Company Name	
Website	
Username	Password
Email	
Phone	Fax
Company Name	
Website	
Username	Password
Email	
Phone	Fax
Company Name	
Website	
Username	Password
Email	
Phone	Fax
Company Name	
Website	
Username	Password
Email	
Phone	Fax
Company Name	
Website	
Username	Password
Email	
Phone	Fax
Company Name	
Website	
Username	Password
Email	
Phone	Fax

Q

Company Name	
Website	
Username	Password
Email	
Phone	Fax

Company Name	
Website	
Username	Password
Email	
Phone	Fax

Company Name	
Website	
Username	Password
Email	
Phone	Fax

Company Name	
Website	
Username	Password
Email	
Phone	Fax

Company Name	
Website	
Username	Password
Email	
Phone	Fax

Company Name	
Website	
Username	Password
Email	
Phone	Fax

R

Company Name

Website

Username   Password

Email

Phone   Fax

Company Name

Website

Username   Password

Email

Phone   Fax

Company Name

Website

Username   Password

Email

Phone   Fax

Company Name

Website

Username   Password

Email

Phone   Fax

Company Name

Website

Username   Password

Email

Phone   Fax

Company Name

Website

Username   Password

Email

Phone   Fax

R

Company Name	
Website	
Username	Password
Email	
Phone	Fax
Company Name	
Website	
Username	Password
Email	
Phone	Fax
Company Name	
Website	
Username	Password
Email	
Phone	Fax
Company Name	
Website	
Username	Password
Email	
Phone	Fax
Company Name	
Website	
Username	Password
Email	
Phone	Fax
Company Name	
Website	
Username	Password
Email	
Phone	Fax

R

Company Name	
Website	
Username	Password
Email	
Phone	Fax

Company Name	
Website	
Username	Password
Email	
Phone	Fax

Company Name	
Website	
Username	Password
Email	
Phone	Fax

Company Name	
Website	
Username	Password
Email	
Phone	Fax

Company Name	
Website	
Username	Password
Email	
Phone	Fax

Company Name	
Website	
Username	Password
Email	
Phone	Fax

R

Company Name	
Website	
Username	Password
Email	
Phone	Fax

Company Name	
Website	
Username	Password
Email	
Phone	Fax

Company Name	
Website	
Username	Password
Email	
Phone	Fax

Company Name	
Website	
Username	Password
Email	
Phone	Fax

Company Name	
Website	
Username	Password
Email	
Phone	Fax

Company Name	
Website	
Username	Password
Email	
Phone	Fax

S

Company Name

Website

Username   Password

Email

Phone   Fax

Company Name

Website

Username   Password

Email

Phone   Fax

Company Name

Website

Username   Password

Email

Phone   Fax

Company Name

Website

Username   Password

Email

Phone   Fax

Company Name

Website

Username   Password

Email

Phone   Fax

Company Name

Website

Username   Password

Email

Phone   Fax

S

Company Name	
Website	
Username	Password
Email	
Phone	Fax

Company Name	
Website	
Username	Password
Email	
Phone	Fax

Company Name	
Website	
Username	Password
Email	
Phone	Fax

Company Name	
Website	
Username	Password
Email	
Phone	Fax

Company Name	
Website	
Username	Password
Email	
Phone	Fax

Company Name	
Website	
Username	Password
Email	
Phone	Fax

S

Company Name	
Website	
Username	Password
Email	
Phone	Fax

Company Name	
Website	
Username	Password
Email	
Phone	Fax

Company Name	
Website	
Username	Password
Email	
Phone	Fax

Company Name	
Website	
Username	Password
Email	
Phone	Fax

Company Name	
Website	
Username	Password
Email	
Phone	Fax

Company Name	
Website	
Username	Password
Email	
Phone	Fax

S

Company Name	
Website	
Username	Password
Email	
Phone	Fax

Company Name	
Website	
Username	Password
Email	
Phone	Fax

Company Name	
Website	
Username	Password
Email	
Phone	Fax

Company Name	
Website	
Username	Password
Email	
Phone	Fax

Company Name	
Website	
Username	Password
Email	
Phone	Fax

Company Name	
Website	
Username	Password
Email	
Phone	Fax

T

Company Name	
Website	
Username	Password
Email	
Phone	Fax

Company Name	
Website	
Username	Password
Email	
Phone	Fax

Company Name	
Website	
Username	Password
Email	
Phone	Fax

Company Name	
Website	
Username	Password
Email	
Phone	Fax

Company Name	
Website	
Username	Password
Email	
Phone	Fax

Company Name	
Website	
Username	Password
Email	
Phone	Fax

T

Company Name	
Website	
Username	Password
Email	
Phone	Fax
Company Name	
Website	
Username	Password
Email	
Phone	Fax
Company Name	
Website	
Username	Password
Email	
Phone	Fax
Company Name	
Website	
Username	Password
Email	
Phone	Fax
Company Name	
Website	
Username	Password
Email	
Phone	Fax
Company Name	
Website	
Username	Password
Email	
Phone	Fax

T

Company Name

Website

Username   Password

Email

Phone   Fax

Company Name

Website

Username   Password

Email

Phone   Fax

Company Name

Website

Username   Password

Email

Phone   Fax

Company Name

Website

Username   Password

Email

Phone   Fax

Company Name

Website

Username   Password

Email

Phone   Fax

Company Name

Website

Username   Password

Email

Phone   Fax

T

Company Name	
Website	
Username	Password
Email	
Phone	Fax

Company Name	
Website	
Username	Password
Email	
Phone	Fax

Company Name	
Website	
Username	Password
Email	
Phone	Fax

Company Name	
Website	
Username	Password
Email	
Phone	Fax

Company Name	
Website	
Username	Password
Email	
Phone	Fax

Company Name	
Website	
Username	Password
Email	
Phone	Fax

U

Company Name	
Website	
Username	Password
Email	
Phone	Fax

Company Name	
Website	
Username	Password
Email	
Phone	Fax

Company Name	
Website	
Username	Password
Email	
Phone	Fax

Company Name	
Website	
Username	Password
Email	
Phone	Fax

Company Name	
Website	
Username	Password
Email	
Phone	Fax

Company Name	
Website	
Username	Password
Email	
Phone	Fax

U

Company Name	
Website	
Username	Password
Email	
Phone	Fax
Company Name	
Website	
Username	Password
Email	
Phone	Fax
Company Name	
Website	
Username	Password
Email	
Phone	Fax
Company Name	
Website	
Username	Password
Email	
Phone	Fax
Company Name	
Website	
Username	Password
Email	
Phone	Fax
Company Name	
Website	
Username	Password
Email	
Phone	Fax

U

Company Name	
Website	
Username	Password
Email	
Phone	Fax

Company Name	
Website	
Username	Password
Email	
Phone	Fax

Company Name	
Website	
Username	Password
Email	
Phone	Fax

Company Name	
Website	
Username	Password
Email	
Phone	Fax

Company Name	
Website	
Username	Password
Email	
Phone	Fax

Company Name	
Website	
Username	Password
Email	
Phone	Fax

U

Company Name	
Website	
Username	Password
Email	
Phone	Fax

Company Name	
Website	
Username	Password
Email	
Phone	Fax

Company Name	
Website	
Username	Password
Email	
Phone	Fax

Company Name	
Website	
Username	Password
Email	
Phone	Fax

Company Name	
Website	
Username	Password
Email	
Phone	Fax

Company Name	
Website	
Username	Password
Email	
Phone	Fax

V

Company Name	
Website	
Username	Password
Email	
Phone	Fax

Company Name	
Website	
Username	Password
Email	
Phone	Fax

Company Name	
Website	
Username	Password
Email	
Phone	Fax

Company Name	
Website	
Username	Password
Email	
Phone	Fax

Company Name	
Website	
Username	Password
Email	
Phone	Fax

Company Name	
Website	
Username	Password
Email	
Phone	Fax

V

Company Name	
Website	
Username	Password
Email	
Phone	Fax

Company Name	
Website	
Username	Password
Email	
Phone	Fax

Company Name	
Website	
Username	Password
Email	
Phone	Fax

Company Name	
Website	
Username	Password
Email	
Phone	Fax

Company Name	
Website	
Username	Password
Email	
Phone	Fax

Company Name	
Website	
Username	Password
Email	
Phone	Fax

V

Company Name	
Website	
Username	Password
Email	
Phone	Fax

Company Name	
Website	
Username	Password
Email	
Phone	Fax

Company Name	
Website	
Username	Password
Email	
Phone	Fax

Company Name	
Website	
Username	Password
Email	
Phone	Fax

Company Name	
Website	
Username	Password
Email	
Phone	Fax

Company Name	
Website	
Username	Password
Email	
Phone	Fax

V

Company Name	
Website	
Username	Password
Email	
Phone	Fax

Company Name	
Website	
Username	Password
Email	
Phone	Fax

Company Name	
Website	
Username	Password
Email	
Phone	Fax

Company Name	
Website	
Username	Password
Email	
Phone	Fax

Company Name	
Website	
Username	Password
Email	
Phone	Fax

Company Name	
Website	
Username	Password
Email	
Phone	Fax

W

Company Name	
Website	
Username	Password
Email	
Phone	Fax

Company Name	
Website	
Username	Password
Email	
Phone	Fax

Company Name	
Website	
Username	Password
Email	
Phone	Fax

Company Name	
Website	
Username	Password
Email	
Phone	Fax

Company Name	
Website	
Username	Password
Email	
Phone	Fax

Company Name	
Website	
Username	Password
Email	
Phone	Fax

W

Company Name	
Website	
Username	Password
Email	
Phone	Fax

Company Name	
Website	
Username	Password
Email	
Phone	Fax

Company Name	
Website	
Username	Password
Email	
Phone	Fax

Company Name	
Website	
Username	Password
Email	
Phone	Fax

Company Name	
Website	
Username	Password
Email	
Phone	Fax

Company Name	
Website	
Username	Password
Email	
Phone	Fax

W

Company Name

Website

Username   Password

Email

Phone   Fax

Company Name

Website

Username   Password

Email

Phone   Fax

Company Name

Website

Username   Password

Email

Phone   Fax

Company Name

Website

Username   Password

Email

Phone   Fax

Company Name

Website

Username   Password

Email

Phone   Fax

Company Name

Website

Username   Password

Email

Phone   Fax

W

Company Name	
Website	
Username	Password
Email	
Phone	Fax

Company Name	
Website	
Username	Password
Email	
Phone	Fax

Company Name	
Website	
Username	Password
Email	
Phone	Fax

Company Name	
Website	
Username	Password
Email	
Phone	Fax

Company Name	
Website	
Username	Password
Email	
Phone	Fax

Company Name	
Website	
Username	Password
Email	
Phone	Fax

X

Company Name	
Website	
Username	Password
Email	
Phone	Fax

Company Name	
Website	
Username	Password
Email	
Phone	Fax

Company Name	
Website	
Username	Password
Email	
Phone	Fax

Company Name	
Website	
Username	Password
Email	
Phone	Fax

Company Name	
Website	
Username	Password
Email	
Phone	Fax

Company Name	
Website	
Username	Password
Email	
Phone	Fax

X

Company Name	
Website	
Username	Password
Email	
Phone	Fax
Company Name	
Website	
Username	Password
Email	
Phone	Fax
Company Name	
Website	
Username	Password
Email	
Phone	Fax
Company Name	
Website	
Username	Password
Email	
Phone	Fax
Company Name	
Website	
Username	Password
Email	
Phone	Fax
Company Name	
Website	
Username	Password
Email	
Phone	Fax

X

Company Name	
Website	
Username	Password
Email	
Phone	Fax

Company Name	
Website	
Username	Password
Email	
Phone	Fax

Company Name	
Website	
Username	Password
Email	
Phone	Fax

Company Name	
Website	
Username	Password
Email	
Phone	Fax

Company Name	
Website	
Username	Password
Email	
Phone	Fax

Company Name	
Website	
Username	Password
Email	
Phone	Fax

X

Company Name	
Website	
Username	Password
Email	
Phone	Fax

Company Name	
Website	
Username	Password
Email	
Phone	Fax

Company Name	
Website	
Username	Password
Email	
Phone	Fax

Company Name	
Website	
Username	Password
Email	
Phone	Fax

Company Name	
Website	
Username	Password
Email	
Phone	Fax

Company Name	
Website	
Username	Password
Email	
Phone	Fax

Y

Company Name	
Website	
Username	Password
Email	
Phone	Fax
Company Name	
Website	
Username	Password
Email	
Phone	Fax
Company Name	
Website	
Username	Password
Email	
Phone	Fax
Company Name	
Website	
Username	Password
Email	
Phone	Fax
Company Name	
Website	
Username	Password
Email	
Phone	Fax
Company Name	
Website	
Username	Password
Email	
Phone	Fax

Y

Company Name	
Website	
Username	Password
Email	
Phone	Fax
Company Name	
Website	
Username	Password
Email	
Phone	Fax
Company Name	
Website	
Username	Password
Email	
Phone	Fax
Company Name	
Website	
Username	Password
Email	
Phone	Fax
Company Name	
Website	
Username	Password
Email	
Phone	Fax
Company Name	
Website	
Username	Password
Email	
Phone	Fax

Y

Company Name	
Website	
Username	Password
Email	
Phone	Fax
Company Name	
Website	
Username	Password
Email	
Phone	Fax
Company Name	
Website	
Username	Password
Email	
Phone	Fax
Company Name	
Website	
Username	Password
Email	
Phone	Fax
Company Name	
Website	
Username	Password
Email	
Phone	Fax
Company Name	
Website	
Username	Password
Email	
Phone	Fax

Y

Company Name	
Website	
Username	Password
Email	
Phone	Fax
Company Name	
Website	
Username	Password
Email	
Phone	Fax
Company Name	
Website	
Username	Password
Email	
Phone	Fax
Company Name	
Website	
Username	Password
Email	
Phone	Fax
Company Name	
Website	
Username	Password
Email	
Phone	Fax
Company Name	
Website	
Username	Password
Email	
Phone	Fax

Z

Company Name

Website

Username   Password

Email

Phone   Fax

Company Name

Website

Username   Password

Email

Phone   Fax

Company Name

Website

Username   Password

Email

Phone   Fax

Company Name

Website

Username   Password

Email

Phone   Fax

Company Name

Website

Username   Password

Email

Phone   Fax

Company Name

Website

Username   Password

Email

Phone   Fax

Z

Company Name	
Website	
Username	Password
Email	
Phone	Fax
Company Name	
Website	
Username	Password
Email	
Phone	Fax
Company Name	
Website	
Username	Password
Email	
Phone	Fax
Company Name	
Website	
Username	Password
Email	
Phone	Fax
Company Name	
Website	
Username	Password
Email	
Phone	Fax
Company Name	
Website	
Username	Password
Email	
Phone	Fax

Z

Company Name

Website

Username   Password

Email

Phone   Fax

Company Name

Website

Username   Password

Email

Phone   Fax

Company Name

Website

Username   Password

Email

Phone   Fax

Company Name

Website

Username   Password

Email

Phone   Fax

Company Name

Website

Username   Password

Email

Phone   Fax

Company Name

Website

Username   Password

Email

Phone   Fax

Z

Company Name	
Website	
Username	Password
Email	
Phone	Fax
Company Name	
Website	
Username	Password
Email	
Phone	Fax
Company Name	
Website	
Username	Password
Email	
Phone	Fax
Company Name	
Website	
Username	Password
Email	
Phone	Fax
Company Name	
Website	
Username	Password
Email	
Phone	Fax
Company Name	
Website	
Username	Password
Email	
Phone	Fax